Women of Devotion

BARBARA B. SMITH
WITH SHIRLEY W. THOMAS

BOOKCRAFT
Salt Lake City, Utah

ISBN 0–88494–735–1

2nd Printing, 1990

Printed in the United States of America

Contents

Introduction

There was a time, not many years ago, when nearly all children were just like me. I would run home from school, throw open the front door, and call, "Mother, where are you?"

"I'm here in the kitchen, making biscuits." Or she might be in the dining room studying for her next seminary presentation, or upstairs tidying the boys' room. But her reassuring answer was the sound that signaled home.

Only occasionally did my call echo back unanswered. When it did I made my way to the kitchen, and there on the table lay a note: "Dear Ones, I've taken Aunt Elsie to the doctor. We should be home about 5:00 P.M. Love, *M* [*M* meant Mother]."

Knowing that Mother was there lent certainty to my day and gave stability to my life. Her infrequent absences, with their attendant notes on the kitchen table, were tolerable only because they were temporary. The comfort I sensed on coming home became a continuing feeling through each day and gave me the confidence to face the unfamiliar and the frightening that are so much a part of a young child's life. Knowing of her presence filled as profound a need as feeling of her love, and to me there was some relationship between the two.

I didn't try to reason out why I needed her so much. I only knew that when she was there I felt secure, loved, wanted, happy. It was that mix of emotions that caused me to hurry home. Home was the embodiment of the characteristics of my parents and, when I was a child, more pervasively those of my mother. I did not understand then that in my mother's presence I felt the righteousness she personified, the attributes of divine love that she had learned to live.

A mother has accepted the responsibility for introducing spirit children to mortality and training them in the ways of earth life. If she has an understanding of our Heavenly Father's plan, she will recognize an even more sobering obligation to help them remember the celestial life from whence they came. Though a veil is drawn over their recollection of a previous sphere, their spirits have been nurtured in a realm of perfect love. A mother will most nearly recreate that climate here for her children as she reflects that goodness.

Before a child is old enough to know and choose for himself, he will have modeled what his mother does and what she is. Her ways are his text, the home she creates, his laboratory. Coming to earth, a newborn baby turns a pristine page in his book of life. His mother has the first opportunity to affect its contents—establishing continuity with the past, influencing direction for the future.

My mother's influence has been felt in my family; I see it yet in the lives of our children. I love to be in the home of a daughter or son and listen as the children come home from school and call, "Mother, where are you?" And I love to hear the answer, "I'm here in the kitchen talking to Grandmother." As I listen I recall my own feelings as a child. It takes me very quickly through generations that I hope will be together forever in the bonds secured by love. The late President J. Reuben Clark echoed my hope in his plea "that our homes shall be so built here that they shall be bathed always in the saving sunshine of God's blessings; that so built here these homes of ours shall grow and ripen into celestial homes of eternity" (J. Reuben Clark, Jr., *Relief Society Magazine,* December 1940, p. 810).

In her basic creation as companion, and in the image of Eve, mother of all living, a woman rises to her place in the Father's plan. She becomes exemplar and teacher of eternal principles. Long before a child can comprehend the life and mission of the Savior, he can learn the selfless qualities of Christlike love as he sees them manifested in his mother.

In my mother's love I felt the radiance of godly love. I see this light also in the lives of other mothers. They, through being Christlike themselves, have introduced their children to his pattern for eternal life. Blessed indeed are children who first learn the ways of the Lord through the tender teachings of their mother's love.

Even brief glimpses into the everyday lives of righteous women can reveal the effect of their goodness on their families. As I have known the wives of members of the First Presidency and the Council of the Twelve, I have seen and appreciated in them beautiful manifestations of the Savior's love. These attributes have made them remarkable mothers.

Flora Amussen Benson

I had just given birth to our second daughter when the nurse came in to announce yet another baby girl, born only minutes after mine. The baby's mother was Sister Flora Benson, wife of the newest member of the Council of the Twelve Apostles.

Sharing such an important time with Sister Benson has caused me to feel more than a casual identification with her. Many times since that warm August night we have talked together, recalling and reliving our experiences. Beyond those talks, however, I have observed Flora Benson with her family and have read about her with particular interest. I have learned from her some valuable lessons about mothering.

Being a mother may begin with bringing a child into mortal life, but it reaches through the continuing responsibility of preparing that child for immortality and eternal life. A mother has a feeling of partnership with our Heavenly Father when her child is born, and there is also a desire to be one with whom he can be pleased. Mothering, of the kind we hope for, means perpetuating righteousness through generations of our Heavenly Father's children.

Sister Benson was brought to the hospital the night of her daughter's birth by her sisters-in-law, Elder Benson being on a Church assignment. A message reached him promptly, however, and he arrived at her bedside shortly before the baby was born. Seeing their mutual respect for one another's needs, I gained a new admiration for the responsibility of mothering and for a wife's role in supporting her husband.

Time and time again through their life together, Sister Benson has made it possible for her husband to accept commitments of great import because she was able to handle matters of the home so capably.

Flora Benson did not leave the teaching of her children to chance experiences or to school alone. She carefully provided learning opportunities for them. Because of Elder Benson's work in the Church and in the government, the family often hosted dignitaries in their home. The children were trained to fulfill many of the duties associated with these occasions, including serving, visiting with, and performing for these guests. They did it with grace and ease.

Perhaps Sister Benson has been concerned most, as a mother, with helping each of the six Benson children find and develop their individual capabilities. Not only has she been totally convinced of the importance of her role, but she has believed at least as strongly in the worth of each one of her children. She has realized that a mother participates in the success of her child by teaching, encouraging, inspiring, correcting, supporting, and, above all else, by loving. There may be nowhere that unconditional love is more important than in a mother.

That this confidence and love was felt and appreciated is evident in the comment by her son Reed. He expresses the feelings of all the children when he says, "Mother was a lifter—an inspirer. Like Abigail Adams, she was a 'yea-sayer.' She would try to discover the potential for good in a person and then encourage them to magnify it. As my father frequently testified, she had more faith in him than he had in himself."

Sister Benson was determined to give her children every opportunity, blessing, protection, and good experience possible for their growth to their fullest potential.

Marjorie Pay Hinckley

President and Sister Hinckley have traveled the world over many times in the fulfillment of President Hinckley's Church assignments. Mother-like, Sister Hinckley has wished that their children could see the beautiful places she and her husband have seen and that they too could come to know and love the people in those far-off lands. Always she has tried to remember those travels and to share her remembrances with the children.

As her daughter Kathleen said, "None of this travel was ever lost on Mother. She absorbed everything she saw and heard. She loved the people she met, and as we learned of them from her, we loved them too. When the Korean sisters wore their native dress for the temple dedication, she remembered their gowns with precision and, through her description, recreated them in detail for us. We experienced each of Mother and Father's trips—the people, the places, the tastes, and the smells—vicariously, through the vivid accounts of our mother."

On the approach of their fiftieth wedding anniversary, President Hinckley asked his wife what she would like as a remembrance of that day. Without hesitation she replied that she would like to take their children to see the places she had longed to show them. The gift was hers. They set a time when President Hinckley would be making a tour of the Far East Area. Their daughter Kathy said that "it was a mountain-moving kind of a project, almost an impossible dream," to make all the arrangements necessary so that the five Hinckley children and their spouses could meet their parents in Hong Kong and travel with them as they completed the Asian tour.

Since my husband was serving as the Area President in Asia, I was privileged to see the Hinckley family on this unforgettable journey. They traveled from one wondrous place to another, and as they did, all the accounts they had heard over the years came to life before their eyes. There, among those people whom President Hinckley had served so long and so loyally, dreams were fulfilled, family memories created; it was a scene dear to any mother's heart. In the sweet interaction that took place in this family, no one was neglected; each was important. On a typical evening, their father would be exhausted after a day of meetings, including the evening meal with local leaders. Their mother would attend to the conversation of her husband and the leaders for a time, then slip quietly away to be sure that all was well with her family.

I could sense in this pattern the careful way that Sister Hinckley has been able, over the years, to respond to the needs of her children while at the same time supporting her husband in his critical role in the work of our Father's kingdom.

Her children have always known that their mother would have time and a sympathetic ear for their concerns. When compassion is called for, she gives it liberally. However, Sister Hinckley often helps her children gain a perspective of their problems that reveals the humor in them. "She laughs us out of many things," says Kathy. "She has that same good humor with the grandchildren. In fact she has such good times with them that they have been known to call her their 'groovy grandma.' "

Providing love and laughter and personal concern, Marjorie Hinckley fulfills her role as mother with a kind of caring that makes each individual feel significant and cherished.

Frances Beverly Johnson Monson

If a boy could choose his mother, he might ask for someone very like Frances Beverly Johnson Monson. Though a woman of feminine tastes, she somehow understands the heart of a boy. For example, when one of her sons wanted to have pigeons—Birmingham Roller pigeons—she let him have them. Not only did she let him have them, but when she knew he was serious about it, she also helped him travel to England, where he became acquainted with the Birmingham Roller specialist of the world. She allowed her other son to keep a pet snake in the bathtub, and on one occasion drove him all over the valley to find the particular quail he wanted to buy as his newest pet. If he wanted the biggest pumpkin in town, or a special tree for his own room at Christmastime, she was happy to help him find it. Moreover, if it happened that her son couldn't get home in time on a particular night, she would feed and water his pets.

The truth is, Frances Monson is a supportive mom.

The Monsons' daughter knows that as well as the two boys do. Although her parents had to be away at times, she had the kind of attention from them that assured her of their love and interest. When she came in from a date or a party, her mother was there, and they usually spent the next few minutes in a late-night chat. Because there was only one girl in the family, Frances Monson and her daughter developed a particular closeness.

Their relationship was a source of strength and comfort when Ann, her husband, and their three children were moving back to the West. It was a major move for this couple, and all of their possessions were packed into a moving van for transit. En route, the vehicle became involved in a serious accident and caught fire, burning the contents completely.

They were a pretty shattered young family when they arrived at the Monson home. After Sister Monson had made them comfortable with food and clean rooms to stay in, she was able to help them gain a perspective about their losses. She let them see that their furniture was replaceable and that even if it were not, no chairs or desks or beds, however valuable, were eternal. Of greater worth, and more to be regretted, was the loss of their marriage and baby's blessing certificates. Sister Monson reminded them that even these are only representative and that the priceless intangibles they stand for cannot be destroyed by fire.

Sister Monson enjoys being close to her children. When they were younger she managed her time in order to be with them as often as she could. She frequently gave up other choice opportunities so that she could be at home when they were there. The children remember particularly that she made what many might call sacrifices for them and for their father without complaining. Her son Clark, as he spoke of her, said more than once, "My mother didn't complain." This is a notable remembrance of childhood for a home in which the husband and father was required by assignment to be away often.

Frances Monson has the useful attitude of enjoying the intensity of the away-from-home world that she and President Monson frequently share and of being content when she is at home. Since she is required to be "on call," often going quickly from one of these situations to the other, it serves her family well that she does it with grace and pleasure. I see in this flexibility the same attitude that enabled her to give her children the freedom to develop their own interests with independence—even if it meant snakes in the bathtub—yet on the other hand give them counsel or guidance or sympathy as it was needed.

President Monson has sometimes spoken of "the miraculous strength and mighty power" in a mother's love and in a child's love for Mother. This is borne out in his own home, where the strength and power of Sister Monson's love for her children and their appreciation for her have combined to provide a bulwark against the hurtful forces of the world.

Clara May Jeffs Hunter

"With her faintly regal manner, I thought she might be a bit aloof. Quite the contrary, however, was true. She was warmly gracious and reacted with interest and concern to a field quite apart from her usual frame of reference." So recalled a Brigham Young University faculty member who, after a presentation he had given a number of years previously, had the opportunity to lunch with Elder and Sister Hunter.

Since Sister Hunter's passing in 1983, memories of her are cherished by persons who were privileged to know her—not only those closest to her, but many also whose lives were only brushed by hers in brief acquaintance.

In my own touch with her life, I could see not only her sensitive, caring attitude but also her love of beauty. It was evident in her home—a place of tasteful surroundings, of refinement and learning—a place abounding in love. She chose carefully and worked tirelessly to create for her family the kind of perfection that gave evidence of the eternal beauty they would one day enjoy.

With her husband, Elder Howard W. Hunter, Sister Hunter endeavored to establish a home built on gospel principles. Together they were devoted to building a righteous family and supporting the work of the Lord. The early grief she suffered at the loss of an infant son was solaced largely by the joy she experienced with their other two sons, John and Richard.

She took a keen interest in their schooling and activities, encouraging them always to achieve their best. Both acknowledge the vital part their mother played in their accomplishments.

John remembers in his mother a remarkable steadfastness. When he and his brother were actively involved in sports—at different schools—she was the one who picked them up and delivered them, taking them where they needed to be when they needed to be there. She did this every day with regularity. Not only did she get them to their practices; she always attended their games. Oftentimes their father was unable to come because of other obligations, but their mother was there cheering them on. John appreciated her when he was a young man, but only now, viewed from his present perspective as a parent, does he realize the truly exceptional nature of all she did.

Another quality of his mother that John looks to as a source of lasting strength in his life was her decisiveness in matters of right and wrong. She never left her sons wondering about her position. This certitude that characterized Clara Hunter's life is reflected now in her sons.

Richard, like John, feels the pervasive influence of his mother in his life. He remembers the "let's-get-it-done" enthusiasm that spurred the action in their home. She was a tireless worker. Through following their mother's model of diligence, they learned the satisfaction of accomplishment. An associated blessing for them as young boys was their experiencing a sense of security in knowing of her approval and their feeling of having lived up to her expectations of them.

As John and Richard have matured, they have extended their own influence through lives of service and successful accomplishment. Yet it might honestly be said that in each of the achievements of her sons may be seen the inevitable imprint of Clara Hunter.

Donna Smith Packer

It was close to the time dinner guests were expected to arrive at the home of Elder Boyd K. Packer and his wife, Donna. Donna and I were chatting as we arranged the place cards. The carefully set tables added to the beauty of the living room and sun room of their ranch-style house. Sister Packer had invited me to become acquainted with their home before we began the task of arranging seating for those invited to dinner that night. I had admired the handmade quilts, the handsomely braided rag rugs, and the lace-edged pillows standing starched against polished brass beds.

Everything I saw seemed special, a kind of memento honoring the past or reflecting the interests and talents of this remarkable family. I had a sense, in this home, of deep family roots. Also present was an aura of harmony. From the kitchen came the occasional laughter of the Packer children, who are now mostly grown. I knew, from her responsive smile and words of appreciation, that, more than rugs or lace edgings or shiny beds, these—her children—were Donna Packer's treasure.

Tonight they had come from as far as several miles or just beyond the back fence to help, as was their wont when any member of the family had a special need. Working together to help family members was not a "rescue operation" but a tradition.

I learned that when the children were all living at home, Sister Packer would organize the work to be done—the yard, the fruit trees, the vegetable garden, and the household chores—and then direct the team action required to accomplish that work.

The teamwork was there in the kitchen that evening, and it constituted a remarkable display of family togetherness. I knew it did not just happen. I believe it was due in large part to the commitment Sister Packer has always had to her role as a mother. She put her children and their training and well-being ahead of every outside-the-home consideration. "When I see our children working together, learning how to manage homes of their own, and facing the problems of family life with reality," says Sister Packer, "I am pleased for that decision. We have been able to teach our children our values."

Remembering his mother's role in their home life, the Packers' son Kenneth reflects that their mother's organizing ability was the key. She developed the sense of teamwork that has become a hallmark of their family effectiveness. "Even now," he says, "if she knows of a need one of us has, she'll call around until others are alerted. Then together we help."

"Our life, however, was not always group related," says Ken. He speaks warmly of one-to-one talks with his mother, whom he finds very easy to talk to.

Also among his choice recollections was the pleasure with which they anticipated coming home from school each day, knowing there would always be hot bread, fresh from the oven, waiting for them on the table. Such an accomplishment on the part of his mother brought him not only pleasure but a sense of admiration too.

His mother's recent publication *On Footings from the Past*, a 467-page compilation of Packer family history from 1460 to 1924, is another cause for admiration. Written from information garnered during years of relentless research, this book gives further evidence of Donna Packer's tireless efforts to support her husband and children and to secure the eternal promises for their family.

Norma Berntson Ashton

In a memorable general conference address, Elder Marvin J. Ashton fixed upon the words *I went home*. He drew from Joseph Smith—History 1:20, which reads: "Soon recovering in some degree, I went home. And as I leaned up to the fireplace, mother inquired what the matter was.'' Elder Ashton pointed out the importance of home to Joseph Smith: that when Joseph was drained physically by the extraordinary spiritual experiences associated with obtaining the plates, he turned first to his home. There at the hearth he received the sympathetic support of his mother.

Hearing his talk, one could sense that Elder Ashton too has known the comfort of a sheltering home. He and his wife, Norma, have four children who now are grown and have their own families; but they love to come ''home.'' And, like Joseph Smith, they will find there the concern of their mother.

As one son describes his mother, ''She is a great listener; she cares about people.'' Both these sought-for qualities make Sister Ashton an understanding mother, one whose home becomes a respite from the world. She understands the distractions of today's children with school, friends, and activities. Knowing of these constraints, Norma Ashton makes very few demands of her children.

However, as her son John says, ''She knows when we are preoccupied, but we also know that once we are with Mother, we have a wise, warm friend who will give us her time and complete attention—or she will be our most challenging competitor.''

The competition he speaks of usually takes place on the tennis court, or sometimes in golf or in any of a number of parlor games, for the Ashtons are fond of playing together. The children all have learned to enjoy playing games, and they are seldom together very long before a game of some sort ''breaks out.'' These activities have established a closeness among the brothers and sisters, but even more, the children have felt a great comradery with their mother and their father.

While recreational activities are given considerable weight in the Ashton scale of preferences, they are greatly outranked by gospel considerations. Theirs is a Church-related home.

Before Elder Ashton was called to be a member of the Council of the Twelve, Sister Ashton served as a member of the Relief Society General Board. Through her service in that position, her children felt that their lives were enriched as she shared with them the training and the great insights into happy living that she received. As a former school teacher, Sister Ashton was always anxious to help her children learn, and she knew that the learning of greatest worth to them was that which would strengthen their testimonies of the gospel of Jesus Christ.

There have been times in the life of Norma Ashton which have tested her faith, such as the serious illness of a young grandson. The family endured anxious months before he overcame a dread disease. Sister Ashton acknowledges with gratitude the hand of a loving Father in Heaven who answered the prayers of hope and faith in behalf of their dear one.

In addition to maintaining the closeness of a loving, friendly home, Norma Ashton has been able to balance her time in order to give service in many community efforts. To these she brings the resource of a continuously trained intellect.

Sister Ashton is a little woman in stature who has a very large heart. She reaches out in love to those about her and has a great capacity for making every person feel comfortable in her presence. She has loved being a mother, and her children have loved her in return. Hers is a quiet, deep love that extends to embrace each child.

Barbara Dayton Perry

Barbara Dayton Perry's sensitivity for recognizing need is matched only by her capacity for responding to it. Attending a luncheon for the wives of General Authorities for the first time is daunting, at best, and presented a particular uneasiness for me. I had known most of the women before, yet in a different setting, and this made me the more unsure of just where I fit in. Barbara Perry, sensing a possible need, came to me quickly and invited me to sit with her. Her warmth made her invitation seem an inevitable one, and our time together was a delight, but that did not dim my awareness of her kindly act and thoughtful concern.

More than once I have been the recipient of her caring regard. I am happy that I have, because it allows me to share fully the deep feelings of other people who know her. One niece says, "She has been just like a mom. I have lived with her. She has shared the financial responsibilities of my life. She takes me out to celebrate my birthday and other special occasions. She even tended my baby for three months while I completed my commitment to my employer. When I would try to thank her, she would say, 'Can't you see how much fun this is for me? I am the one who appreciates the privilege of being with this beautiful infant.' "

Is it any wonder that she has a devoted following? A family of nieces and nephews call her their own.

As a respected faculty member in the Brigham Young University School of Nursing, Sister Perry was especially effective in helping students through a very demanding program. Many who were fearful or discouraged needed the academic help and moral support she was willing to give. With Barbara Dayton's gentle but realistic guidance, a young woman could organize her hours, recognize her potential, take heart, and try again.

Barbara had a new kind of opportunity for sharing when she married Elder L. Tom Perry. Although marriage has brought a different focus to her life, she was already practiced in the essential role of caring. It was as if the Lord had prepared her for this experience. She wanted to bring peace and happiness to the children of Elder Perry. She knew that she could not take the place of their mother, who had passed away, yet she realized there was a very important mothering role to be performed.

One needs to be around the Perry family only a short time to be aware of the blessing Barbara Perry was prepared to bring into that home. It takes a very special kind of woman to love and mother children of another, but she was trained in that art. Long before she married she had learned how to reach out and lift others from sickness, from tragedy, and from loss.

Sister Perry has never been without the joy and fulfillment of mothering. As a nurse she has been professionally trained to extend life. But she does more than that; she enriches the life of every person she knows, young or old. She has a very special way of making each one feel that he or she is her favorite person.

That radiance of spirit has warmed hundreds as she and Elder Perry have traveled throughout the Church on his assignments. Wherever the Perrys have gone, missionaries have been heartened by her caring about each one, one by one. She has been a blessing to Relief Society sisters too. I have observed that they brighten at her very specific appreciation for the foods they have prepared. This allows them to relate to her, individually, in return. It is difficult to measure the value of such interactions, however brief, when they are accompanied by her sincerity and affectionate concern.

In all facets of her life, Barbara Perry has demonstrated the finest of mothering skills. She has learned what many have yet to know: that happiness will come to a woman to the degree that she strives to aid in the cause of righteousness and to nurture and care for others.

Ruby Olson Haight

One time as Sister Ruby Haight, her son, and her granddaughter were horseback riding, the little girl's horse suddenly lurched and began running away. As she passed her father, she screamed, "Help me, Daddy, help me!" The son cried, "Mother, what do I do?" "*Pray*," Sister Haight said.

"Mother, I've already done that," he called back.

They were thankful that the day did not end in tragedy. But it remains for Ruby Haight a lasting reminder of the power of persistent, steady living of the gospel as preparation for the urgency of unexpected need. Sister Haight said that she could not remember teaching her son to pray in time of great need, and certainly the possibility of a runaway horse had not been considered. "But we consistently had our family prayers and blessings on the food, helped the children with their personal prayers, asked for healing in times of sickness—the things that we all do." It was living the practice of prayer each day that made her son approach the Lord for help at this critical time.

The seemingly small things, done daily, have great import for children. As they are learning so many things, those repeated consistently will be remembered best and most likely become established patterns.

As a mother of young children, Sister Haight also felt that daily housekeeping tasks served an important purpose. Not only are they necessary for keeping the home inviting but also they are a prime instrument of mothering. She remembers her daughter, Karen, helping to put clean sheets on the beds. As most mothers know, this is not the most efficient way to get through the morning's duties, yet some of Ruby Haight's sweetest memories are of Karen snapping the sheets over the bed, sending them sailing high, watching them billow down, then saying gleefully, "Oh, this is so much fun! I just love to help make the beds."

They did get the beds made, if not as fast as Sister Haight might have done them alone. More important, though, Karen had been able to experience a little bit of the joy a mother feels in being able to provide comfort for her family.

Sister Haight feels that a mother must recognize the innate goodness in each child if she is to help him recognize that worth in himself; and thus that mother can encourage him to develop to the fullest his God-given capabilities. When holding her first granddaughter Sister Haight felt strength in the purity of a child newly come from our Heavenly Father. This happened not in a nursery, as one might expect, but in a busy place that could hardly be considered suitable for meditative thinking. All around there was noise—cars honking, tires screeching, motors running—but as she held the baby and looked down at her, she was completely unaware of anything else. She could see in the infant that she held in her arms tangible witness of the goodness of our Heavenly Father and his enduring power. She remembers thinking, "I have in my arms another generation. Life goes on; it is eternal."

Seeing the role of mother in an eternal perspective has helped Ruby Haight. A mother often thinks of her work as being undone as fast as she can finish it—the dishes, the clothes, the floors. In perspective, however, these are only the *tasks* of a mother. The *work* she is doing is of unending import. Who can know the reach of a truth implanted, a love secured, and a value instilled? Shaping attitudes and establishing true principles for living are the inestimable, unending results of a mother's work.

Ruth Wright Faust

It has been said of Ruth Wright Faust that she is like the wise man: She "heareth these sayings of [the Lord], and doeth them" (see Matt. 7:24).

Sister Faust's son tells of the influence President Harold B. Lee had in their lives with his counsel to "act as if you have a certain attribute and it will be yours."

"Mother acted the attributes she prized, and they were indeed hers. She paid the price. We honor her for this great lesson she continues to teach. I remember well the pies she made. Mother would make five pies at a time and give away four of them. We children thought she should keep four and give away one. But she could not be dissuaded, because she knew that whatever the need she was trying to meet, she had to give freely. She felt it important to give of both her time and her substance. It was the price of compassionate service."

Without realizing it, Ruth Faust was imbuing her children with her philosophy that the extent to which you give of yourself determines the depth of your sincerity in charitable service. Her children now emulate their mother and are especially anxious that their children learn what she has taught them of the importance of filling another's need.

Sister Faust herself has said, "I love being a mother! I know that becoming a mother was a gift directly given to me by the Lord, and I wanted to treat my children in a way that would be acceptable to him. I want to live so that nothing negative or hurtful will come into the lives of my children that would be the result of my actions. I know that I can control to some extent their future. Each child sent into our home is different, unique, and wonderful, in spite of us."

They watched her as she served as the Relief Society president of their ward, giving years of happy service.

They knew that in those years Sister Faust found it difficult to stand and express in words her love for the Lord. She turned rather to her culinary talents to bless others and to speak her devotion. Even then, however, her children knew the emotional and spiritual maturity of their mother, and it was a source of strength to them.

More recently, Ruth Faust has added a new dimension to the concern she manifests. Much of her reaching out is done in person-to-person conversations. She believes that having an influence on children or grandchildren requires a one-to-one relationship with each individual. This does not happen in an instant; it is the result of constant and continuing contacts. She states, "The right to communicate heart-to-heart with each child and grandchild must be earned."

Even though her family members are now miles apart, she still tries to take an active interest in each one, often communicating by telephone. Even with the busiest of schedules she has found that a telephone call to keep in touch can make a great deal of difference with her children and grandchildren. It doesn't take long to find out the score of a football game a grandson plays. Ruth Faust is one who gives the special effort by making those telephone calls. She knows that sometimes it is just that special moment they share that can help her loved ones stay close to the Lord.

At one time the price of her charity was pies. Now it may be a telephone call. But always, in whatever she does, she is a doer of the word.

That her loved ones are anxious for those moments is evident in the comment of her son: "A brief time with her, and we know that she shares in our joys, hopes, sorrows, and successes, and that she has a sense of forgiveness. All are such an essential part of charity and service!"

Colleen Hinckley Maxwell

Colleen Hinckley Maxwell was in my Gleaner class when she was a teenager. Even then she had the attributes of selflessness so essential to charity, or Christlike love—qualities rarely seen in one of such a young age, highly prized in one of any age.

I saw her little in the years that followed until one night when one of her daughters was participating in a Christmas homemaking activity.

Her daughter had submitted her mother's recipe for shortbread and had prepared a sample for each of the more than one hundred women attending that night. She was lovely and the shortbread delicious, but it was her mother's manner I noted most. She had come to the meeting in order to be supportive of her daughter, not to draw attention to herself as a wife of an Apostle. As I watched her, I could see that she exhibited those same beautiful qualities I had known in her earlier, only they were now more deeply ingrained.

Being supportive of her children has long been a manifestation of Colleen Maxwell's love. Her daughter Becky will always remember the time before a school dance she was to attend. Her mother was making a dress for her to wear and needed to finish it before going to bed that night, however long it might take. Sister Maxwell worked far into the night. Then, in the early hours, the sewing machine broke. Rather than disappoint her daughter, she stayed up all that night and finished the dress, sewing entirely by hand.

Of course, a daughter would never forget such a night. Similarly, each of the other Maxwell children have nights or days, many of them, that they remember because of the extraordinary expressions of their mother's love. She seems to anticipate their needs. Often, now that her children are grown, she will take the grandchildren to her home when she knows the parents have special responsibilities, or even if she thinks they need a break. The grandchildren also look forward to birthdays, at which time each child has the privilege of going shopping and to lunch alone with their grandmother. This one-on-one time is anticipated long before "the day" and treasured long after.

Her children most often think of Colleen Maxwell as a person who reaches out to others with loving concern. Her caring does not stop with her own family. Family members recall the Maxwell dinner table, frequently expanded to accommodate others—a widow or a widower, a newcomer, or simply someone who was lonely. In her sincere concern she gave them a kind of mothering that renewed and encouraged. Her son, Cory, was accustomed to coming home to some delicious-smelling food cooking in the oven, then realizing it was probably for some person in need. Her children admire this quality in their mother.

Her children also admire her learning and wisdom. Cory remembers that the weeks before he left on his mission were particularly rewarding because of the opportunity he had for lengthy conversations with his mother. He found that in addition to her other accomplishments, she had quietly devoted time to the study of the scriptures. She deeply considered their significance and had answers, explanations, and perceptive, thoughtful comments. These lessons were of strength to him. Not unlike the stripling warriors, he was fortified with the I-never-doubted-my-mother-knew-it assurance. Perhaps this is Colleen Hinckley Maxwell's greatest contribution to her family and to others: through her example they find faith and courage to meet the challenges of their own lives.

Dantzel White Nelson

"We had all come home for Christmas," relates Dantzel Nelson's daughter. "Nine of us and our families had more than filled the house with people. One of the little toddlers who was barely able to touch a tabletop reached up and grasped a scarf that was the base for the Lladro porcelain nativity set Mother had put out for the Yuletide season. As that little hand pulled, the elegant, expensive figures fell, crashing to the floor. Three of them broke.

"Aghast, we all instinctively turned to Mother. There was not a sign, not a look, not a motion to indicate that it mattered. At that critical moment she was just as calm and caring as though nothing ruinous had happened.

"It was through her example that she taught us the importance of people. In this instance it was the baby, the parents, the siblings, and all of us who were her concern."

Her sincere caring draws Dantzel Nelson's family to her. They love to come home and look forward to the monthly birthday parties, complete with a big dinner and ample cake and ice cream. For Thanksgiving, they all gather at their mountain home in Midway, Utah, for a full family day. They relax in their big indoor "tub-spa" and bask in the warmth of being all together again.

Another time they like to go to Midway is for Swiss Days—that event which honors the founding fathers of the quaint little village. They also go there on July the Fourth and, true to Sister Nelson's memory-making penchant, she helps the little grandchildren decorate their bicycles and tricycles and create their own Fourth of July parade instead of simply watching it.

The New Year's Eve puzzle has become a tradition with the Nelsons. Sometime during the evening each person works for a while at putting some pieces in, and then, as the time grows late, they all race to finish it before the new year arrives.

Whatever the family activity, Dantzel likes to make it memorable. Her hand so often adds a special touch to make the difference that will heighten the joy of the moment and add to the promise of the future.

Dantzel Nelson has a lovely singing voice, but it is almost as though she is making "beautiful music" with all that she does. Perhaps one thing that creates that sense of loveliness about her is her love of babies—her own ten and now her thirty-eight grandchildren. She loves taking the time to hold and rock them, and they respond to her gentle caress.

That gentleness is reflected also in her children as they have grown older and even in their own families. Dantzel Nelson has succeeded in making more than memories. She has contributed in a substantial way to the happiness of babies of other generations whom she may not hold and rock, but who will be nurtured in happy homes that are a reflection of her modeling the peaceful ways of the Lord.

June Dixon Oaks

The warmth and the relaxed manner of June Dixon Oaks, qualities that make others feel comfortable in her presence and welcome in her home, almost belie the tenacity and determination with which she pursues a goal she has set. These usually contrasting traits combine to make her a particularly effective mother.

Growing up as the daughter of a successful banker, she was accustomed to more privileges than most were in her hometown of Spanish Fork, Utah. But her easygoing, yet determined, way made the transition to the sometimes Spartan life-style of a student wife seem natural. Even when they went to Chicago in order for her husband, Elder Dallin H. Oaks, to pursue a law degree, and they lived in the barracks that served as married students' housing, she was undaunted. With her husband immersed in the demanding schedule of professional training, Sister Oaks took the major responsibility for their growing family of small children. She managed not only to provide happily for their needs but also to engage in her own studies, often by correspondence, finally earning her baccalaureate degree.

This capacity to create an easy atmosphere, and at the same time to achieve difficult tasks, has served her children well. They have had good times together, with stores of happy memories, yet they have succeeded in reaching significant academic attainments, with all the self-discipline such training requires.

While the six Oaks children are all talented and accomplished, the youngest, Jennie, is musically gifted. Sister Oaks knew of Jennie's gift and the responsibility she had as her mother to help develop that talent. Mothering talented children takes days, weeks, months—even years—of dedicated effort. It requires an immense investment of time for listening, practicing, correcting, and accompanying, also taking to and from lessons and performances. It requires faith in the child when she has little faith in herself. Many important events must be forgone as part of the cost of nurturing the talent of a gifted child.

To do all of this, yet help the other children continue in their growth and achievement, required considerable mothering. In addition, the Oaks family, during much of that time, was living in the president's home at Brigham Young University, and Sister Oaks was carrying the weighty responsibilities of president's wife. How well she succeeded is evident in the comments of daughters TruAnn and Cheri.

When asked, "Is there something that comes quickly to mind when you think of your mother?" TruAnn replied, "Oh, yes, she's my best friend! I even used to let my closest girlfriend know that my mother was *really* my best friend. I remember that I would tell her that I couldn't play anymore when I had a chance to go with my mother, even to the grocery store.

"Life could be a bit lonely living in that house [on University Hill], but she made it kind of wonderful. Everything I did became exciting when I rehearsed it to my mother. She was so interested in each detail, in every comment and reaction, that in the end she helped me see what a really extraordinary time it had been."

Unaware of TruAnn's reply, but responding to the same question, daughter Cheri answered, "Well, the first thing I would say is that she is my best friend." Then she continued to tell of how her mother always seemed to know her concerns and to be there when she needed her. She talked of the good fun they had together and the serious times.

These two daughters have expressed some of what all her children could say about the understanding, sensitive, caring nature of June Oaks, a nature that is complemented by her firm, indomitable faith.

Barbara Bowen Ballard

"Mom is really a coach to us," says her daughter, Brynne. "She used to help us through difficulties at school, and now she does the same with our little children.

"I'll always remember the advice she gave me when I was in high school and having a problem which threatened my relationship with my best friend. Hurtful things were said; still, Mother advised, 'No matter what is said about you, don't find yourself saying those kinds of things in return.' It wasn't easy counsel to follow, because retaliation would seem to be such a good answer, but I did what she said. It worked then, and I have always found it to be the best way."

That Barbara Ballard counseled her children to be kind is not surprising because kindness is a quality that is mentioned often when a person describes Sister Ballard. The children remember the related elements of love, patience, and a quiet way. These are methods Barbara Ballard has used with her children and encourages them to practice now with their children.

"Mother never raised her voice in the home," Brynne recalls. "Actually, she didn't need to. Rather, when a difficulty arose, she would carefully analyze to find out what the true problem was, then follow through with calmness to solve it."

One such situation occurred when Elder Ballard was called to preside over the Canada Toronto Mission. He and Sister Ballard had a consuming amount of work to do, but the children, who had been engaged in numberless interesting activities at home, felt uprooted and without friends or purpose to their lives.

Sister Ballard realized the problem and sensed that they needed to be involved in the mission. She talked with her husband, and soon the children were scheduled for interviews with the mission president and were involved in preparing weekly reports, as every good missionary does, and observing personal study time religiously each morning. Before very long, they had the spirit of the mission. Thus integrated, they became excited with what their parents were doing.

The children appreciated their mother's asking for their input on problems she had to resolve. Often their suggestions were followed, and because they were, the children grew in self-confidence.

One has the sense that people are valued in this home. Sister Ballard makes a special effort to openly appreciate her husband. She wants the children to honor his Church position. She realizes they could easily slip into being casual about it, at great loss to them all. They take time to consider the implications of his conference talks in their lives. They have learned to accept the responsibilities of being worthy of his calling.

The esteem they have for each other—children for parents and parents for children—is expansive. When asked if she ever sees herself doing things she saw her mother do, Brynne answered, "Very often, and when I do I am happy. I want to be the kind of mother Mom is to us." This might be the finest return on an investment a mother can have.

Elisa Rogers Wirthlin

"She rarely raised her voice, so when she did, we knew she really meant business," says Elizabeth of her mother, Elisa Rogers Wirthlin. Elizabeth—"Liz," as she is called—is one of the eight children of Elisa Wirthlin and her husband, Elder Joseph B. Wirthlin.

Rearing a family of eight children can be a test for anyone's patience, yet gentleness is perhaps the first characteristic people observe in Sister Wirthlin's relationship with her children. It may be that her quiet persuasion was effective because her love was manifested in such obvious ways.

Liz continues: "Since we were a family of eight children, we didn't have a lot of extras. There were seven girls, and my mom would spend hours at the sewing machine to see that we had all the clothes we needed. In those days, Mom had only a few dresses for herself. But we figured out one year how many she had sewn for us. It was right around ninety-eight."

I think of the lovely string ensemble composed of Wirthlin daughters that has played so beautifully at several programs I have attended. When I think of the part a mother plays in every note a child performs, that number of dresses becomes even more astonishing.

Music seems appropriate to mention when speaking of Sister Wirthlin as a mother, for she has created a home of culture and beauty. But more important, it is a household of faith. Beginning with her own unwavering testimony, Elisa Wirthlin has striven to maintain that spiritual peace that she knows attends those who put their lives in the hands of the Lord. She desired her son and daughters to have a clearly defined system of gospel values and practices that would fortify them for life outside the sheltering love of home. Her children are grateful for her training and remember their mother's counsel that prayer is still the surest link to their Father in Heaven.

Her children have noted the support Sister Wirthlin has given their father. He has served over the years in Church callings that have required heavy time commitments. Not only has his Church service been demanding but also, through the years, his business has required fourteen-hour days six days a week. "Mom took a heavy load, with a big family to raise, and never once complained," says one daughter. It was not Elisa Wirthlin's nature to complain.

Elisa Wirthlin's world is built on a broad perspective, one that allows important happenings to be enjoyed, suffered, participated in, learned from, but not complained about. There is a happy spirit that characterizes Elisa's mothering. The daughters describe the "quiet dignity" of their mother, and add that they would like to give to their children her kind of "settled happiness."

Jeanene Watkins Scott

In speaking at a Brigham Young University women's conference, Jeanene Scott, the wife of Elder Richard G. Scott, said, "I know that as we live close to the Lord, keep his commandments, pray for individual guidance and inspiration, obey the counsel of our living prophets, we can . . . have courage to face life's challenges." She speaks out of the knowledge of experience. Not only does she fulfill the qualifying requirements of receiving the Lord's blessings, but Jeanene Scott has had to "face life's challenges" in a way that many women have not. Early in their married life, they lost a baby who was born prematurely. Six weeks later their very young son, Richard, died during heart surgery. As she counsels women that courage will come, we can believe in her witness.

If Jeanene Scott is a woman of courage, she is also an exemplar of faith. She knows that the Lord speaks to us through a living prophet and that in recent times President Ezra Taft Benson has given specific counsel to women who are mothers: "Teach your children the gospel in your own home, at your own firesides." Even though there were hard times, she always chose to be at home with their children rather than to work in her professional field.

The Scotts have five living children, and Sister Scott has felt a particular urgency to teach them gospel principles and to help them understand how these relate to their lives. She believes that children must learn early in life to be responsible for making decisions and then living with the consequences.

Because of the totality of Jeanene's concern for the rearing of her children, life in the Scott household can best be described as happy and positive—or, as some have said, "positively happy." Indeed, Jeanene Scott is a believer in fun for families. She was taught from childhood not to take herself too seriously and has followed that same approach with her own family. They have learned that family home evening can be held whenever they can all be together. Often, only the briefest time when Elder Scott could be home has become a family event as together they have crunched through the autumn leaves along the Potomac or played in the winter snows of Utah. Such times as these become the happy memories they love to recall.

Jeanene's mother exerted a very positive influence in her life, teaching her by both precept and example. In one important instance, she said, "Jeanene, you are marrying a man who will give a lot of public and Church service. You must do all you can to help him so that he can give himself to the important work he will be asked to do. Prepare yourself to do anything you can to lift his load." Her mother counseled from the perspective of having grown up with a father who was a mission president for twenty years and from having encouraged her husband, who served for seventeen years as a stake president and later for twelve years as a United States senator.

That counsel remains a valuable guide for Sister Scott. "When we cannot clearly see how it will all work out, but act in faith and trust in the Lord, we give him the opportunity to bless our lives. Those who must see the end from the beginning often do not qualify for the Lord's help," said Sister Scott, who is herself a mother who walks by faith, trusting in the Lord.

Conclusion

The Lord called Emma, wife of the Prophet Joseph, an "elect lady" (see D&C 25:3). A word having to do with choice is an appropriate description for the life of a righteous woman, mother of a happy family, for such a life is the result of innumerable right decisions. To be elect, in the sense of which we speak, refers not to popularity or plurality but to what one chooses to stand for.

I see these women standing strong beside their husbands, "not unequally yoked" (see 2 Cor. 6:14). Their strength, however, is most obviously manifested in the form of gentle, kindly expressions of love.

For many years I served in the national organization that annually selects the American Mother of the Year. Through an extensive review process, many women who have positively affected their families and communities are considered for this honor. As I participated in the program, I was impressed by the magnitude of this effort. It is reflective of the almost universal desire to give appropriate recognition to the contributions mothers have made to our lives.

In honoring some, we call attention to all women. I have been blessed to associate with multitudes of them, good women, diverse in many ways. Yet I have noticed that, no matter what her role in this life, each woman, to the degree that she understands the truth of her eternal nature, manifests concern for nurturing others. "Faithful daughters" of "our glorious Mother Eve" (D&C 138:39), they recognize the role of women to help every child realize the divinity inherent in his creation. It is, for every woman, a glorious mission, a transcendent heritage.